Personal, Learning & Thinking Skills in PSHE

Effective Participators

Eileen Osborne
& Steph Yates

Folens

Acknowledgements

p. 40 – The RugMark logo is reproduced with kind permission from RugMark UK; p. 42 – the Fairtrade logo is reproduced with kind permission from the Fairtrade Foundation and the Ethical Consumer Magazine Best Buy logo is reproduced with kind permission from ethicalconsumer.org

United Kingdom: Folens Publishers, Waterslade House, Thame Road, Haddenham, Buckinghamshire, HP17 8NT.
Email: folens@folens.com Website: www.folens.com

Ireland: Folens Publishers, Greenhills Road, Tallaght, Dublin 24.
Email: info@folens.ie Website: www.folens.ie

Editor: Louise Clark
Series designer and layout: Fiona Webb
Illustrations: **Catherine Ward:** 9, 12, 15, 17, 18, 19, 21, 22, 24, 32, 34, 35, 39, 41, 42, 47, 50, 54, 56, 59, 62, 64; Fiona Webb: 11; **Bridget Dowty of GCI:** 23, 29, 38, 46 (bottom), 48; **Sarah Wimperis of GCI**: 46 (top, left and right).
Cover design: Form (www.form.uk.com)

For general spellings Folens adheres to *Oxford Dictionary of English*, Second Edition (Revised), 2005.

First published 2009 by Folens Limited.

ISBN 978-1-85008-454-9   Folens code FD4549

Contents

'The personal, learning and thinking skills (PLTS) framework supports young people in their learning across the curriculum. The skills should be developed through a range of experiences and subject contexts.'

(QCA)

This series, PLTS in PSHE, uses the PLTS framework as a linking bridge to the PSHE programmes of study. It provides a context for PSHE departments to contribute to the overall PLTS skills and competencies, and in doing so provides students with the ability to transfer what they have learnt in PSHE across other curriculum areas.

This is one of six books in the series and each book links to one of the six groups of skills in the PLTS framework. This book has as its focus 'effective participators'.

EFFECTIVE PARTICIPATORS

Focus

Young people actively engage with issues that affect them and those around them. They play a full part in the life of their school, college, workplace or wider community by taking responsible action to bring improvements for others as well as themselves.

Skills, behaviours and personal qualities

Young people:

◎ discuss issues of concern, seeking resolution where needed
◎ present a persuasive case for action
◎ propose practical ways forward, breaking these down into manageable steps
◎ identify improvements that would benefit others as well as themselves
◎ try to influence others, negotiating and balancing diverse views to reach workable solutions
◎ act as advocates for views and beliefs that may differ from their own.

© Qualifications and Curriculum Authority

Throughout the book students are encouraged to be effective participators by engaging with various issues. They are encouraged to look at issues which affect not only themselves but those around them in the wider community, both in school and outside it. One important aspect of *Effective Participators* is that students learn to take responsible action in bringing about improvements. This book is divided into units for Key Stage 3 and Key Stage 4.

Teacher's notes

Each unit has accompanying Teacher's Notes which give information on the unit, and ideas on how to use the Activity Sheets, starters and plenaries. Each unit has its own set of objectives set out in the Teacher's Notes.

Assessment/Progress sheets

On pages 6–7 there are two sheets which focus on student progress and learning. The two sheets can be used to assess progress, decide on targets and help students to move to a higher level in their learning.

	Unit 1: A greener school	Unit 2: The respect agenda	Unit 3: Staying safe – drugs	Unit 4: Break time map	Unit 5: What can you do?	Unit 6: Our money pays for this	Unit 7: There's something wrong	Unit 8: Health and safety audit	Unit 9: Advocacy	Unit 10: Where else?
PSHE Programmes of Study for England	Economic wellbeing and financial capability: 1.4 Economic understanding	Personal wellbeing: 1.5 Diversity	Personal wellbeing: 1.2 Healthy lifestyles	Personal wellbeing: 1.5 Diversity	Personal wellbeing: 1.1 Personal identities	Economic wellbeing and financial capability: 1.4 Economic understanding	Personal wellbeing: 1.2 Healthy lifestyles	Personal wellbeing: 1.3 Risk	Personal wellbeing: 1.4 Relationships	Personal wellbeing: 1.1 Personal identities
Curriculum for Excellence for Scotland	Social studies: People, place and environment	Health and wellbeing: Mental, emotional, social and physical wellbeing	Health and wellbeing: Substance misuse	Health and wellbeing: Mental, emotional, social and physical wellbeing	Social studies: People in society, economy and business	Social studies: People in society, economy and business	Health and wellbeing: Mental, emotional, social and physical wellbeing	Health and wellbeing: Mental, emotional, social and physical wellbeing	Health and wellbeing: Planning for choices and changes	Health and wellbeing: Planning for choices and changes
Personal and Social Education Framework for Wales	Sustainable development and global citizenship	Active citizenship	Health and emotional wellbeing	Health and emotional wellbeing	Active citizenship	Sustainable development and global citizenship	Health and emotional wellbeing	Health and emotional wellbeing	Health and emotional wellbeing	Health and emotional wellbeing
Revised Curriculum for Northern Ireland: Learning for Life and Work	Learning for Life and Work: Local and global citizenship	Learning for Life and Work: Personal development	Learning for Life and Work: Personal development	Learning for Life and Work: Personal development	Learning for Life and Work: Local and global citizenship	Learning for Life and Work: Local and global citizenship	Learning for Life and Work: Personal development	Learning for Life and Work: Local and global citizenship	Learning for Life and Work: Personal development	Learning for Life and Work: Personal development
Every Child Matters	Make a positive contribution	Make a positive contribution	Stay safe	Enjoy and achieve	Make a positive contribution	Be healthy; Stay safe	Be healthy	Stay safe	Make a positive contribution	Enjoy and achieve
Social and Emotional Aspects of Learning	Social skills	Managing feelings	Social skills	Social skills	Motivation	Empathy	Empathy	Social skills	Empathy	Social skills

Effective Participators

Tick the box to show what applies to you at the start of the unit
and then again at the end.

I can...

	At the start of this unit			At the end of this unit		
	🙂	😐	🙁	🙂	😐	🙁
discuss issues of concern and look for solutions when needed						
present a persuasive case for action						
propose practical ways forward						
show initiative, commitment and perseverance and break these down into manageable steps						
identify improvements that would benefit others as well as myself						
influence others for the good						
negotiate and balance different views to reach workable solutions						
speak up for others and defend their views even when different from my own						
play a full part in the life of my school and wider community						

My targets at the end of this unit are:

1 _____

_____

2 _____

_____

3 _____

_____

Effective Participators

You have now assessed how effective a participator you are. This sheet is for you to see how you can progress and improve in the skills needed to be an effective participator. Each statement indicates what you should do to move to being a good or an excellent effective participator.

◎ **I can discuss issues of concern and look for solutions when needed.**
   I must make sure I can discuss in a meaningful and informed way.
   I must learn how to look for solutions.

◎ **I can present a persuasive case for action.**
   I must make sure I can present a persuasive argument.
   I must accept that my argument may not always persuade others to my thinking.

◎ **I can propose practical ways forward.**
   I must understand that not all my proposals are practical.
   I must accept that some of my forward suggestions may not appear 'forward' to others.

◎ **I can show initiative, commitment and perseverance and break these down into manageable steps.**
   I must understand that commitment and perseverance will take up my own time.
   I must understand what 'manageable steps' means and plan accordingly.

◎ **I can identify improvements that would benefit others as well as myself.**
   I must understand that I need to think of others as well as myself.
   I must have confidence in my ability to identify improvements.

◎ **I can influence others for the good.**
   I must understand the difference between good and bad influences.
   I must learn to make sure that my influence on others is positive.

◎ **I can negotiate and balance different views to reach workable solutions.**
   I must understand that there are always different views about problems/issues.
   I must learn to negotiate with others and listen to their views.

◎ **I can speak up for others and defend their views even when different from my own.**
   I must accept that everyone has the right to their own view and opinion.
   I must learn to stand up for the right of others to put forward their views.

◎ **I can play a full part in the life of my school and wider community.**
   I must look for opportunities to help out in my school and community.
   I must understand the commitment this will mean in terms of time and energy.

Teacher's Notes

Objectives

By the end of the lesson, students will:

◎   have found ways of saving resources within school.

◎   have presented a persuasive case for action.

◎   be able to propose practical ways forward, breaking these down into manageable steps.

Prior knowledge

None.

Links

Personal, Social, Health and Economic Education Programmes of Study for England: Economic wellbeing and financial capability: 1.4 Economic understanding.

Curriculum for Excellence for Scotland: Social studies: People, place and environment.

Personal and Social Education Framework for Wales: Sustainable development and global citizenship.

Revised Curriculum for Northern Ireland: Learning for Life and Work: Local and global citizenship.

Background

Schools are being increasingly encouraged to save resources, both as a way of saving money and as part of being responsible members of their communities. The government website www.teachernet.gov.uk/sustainableschools has a number of ideas on schools becoming more environmentally friendly

Starter activity

Ask students to list sources of energy. Someone will probably suggest 'electricity'. Use this as an opportunity to explain that electricity has to be generated from an energy source; it is not an energy source in itself.

Activity sheets

Activity sheet **1.1 What Do You Use?** gets students thinking about the resources which are used in their school. You can then focus on paper, using Activity sheet **1.2 The Paper Mountain**, or energy, using Activity sheet **1.3 Power Drain**, or use both sheets to cover both aspects.

Activity sheet **1.3** requires students to carry out research, and will probably involve them talking to the school's finance officer. As you will not want dozens of students asking the finance officer the same questions, you could give this sheet to one small group while the rest of the class work on Activity sheet **1.2** in class.

Students then need to work in small groups of three or four to plan and carry out their research and campaigns using Activity sheets **1.4 Making Savings** and **1.5 Action Plan**. Activity sheet **1.5** includes an example which you might want to talk through with the students before each group writes its own action plan. Ideas need not be as ambitious as the one in the example; students might simply decide to put up posters reminding people to switch off lights.

Plenary

Work out roughly what savings one of their campaigns has made or might make (for example, three loaves of bread might be saved each day if fewer sandwiches are wasted). Multiply this by 4,200 to find out the savings that could be made if every state secondary school in the UK took the same action.

1.1 What Do You Use?

Look at each of the items below and write down what resources have gone into making and delivering each one to your school. The first one has been done for you.

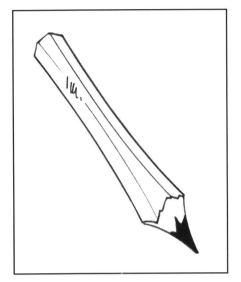

Wood, graphite, paint or dye, glue, cardboard (for packing), electricity to run factory, petrol/diesel for transporting

How many of these resources have you wasted today?

1.2 The Paper Mountain

Schools in developed countries often use huge amounts of paper. In order to save resources, we need to

◎ **reduce** the amount we use

◎ **reuse** where possible

◎ **recycle** when we have finished with it.

How could you reduce, reuse and recycle paper in your school? Use the chart below to write down your ideas. Some ideas have been included to get you started.

Reduce:
Use space sensibly when writing in exercise books.

Reuse:
Cover textbooks to make them last longer.

Recycle:
Have a paper recycling bin in every classroom.

1.3 Power Drain

In the UK, electricity is generated from gas, coal, nuclear power and renewable sources (for example, wind or wave power). The chart below shows the proportion of resources used to create electricity in the UK in 2006.

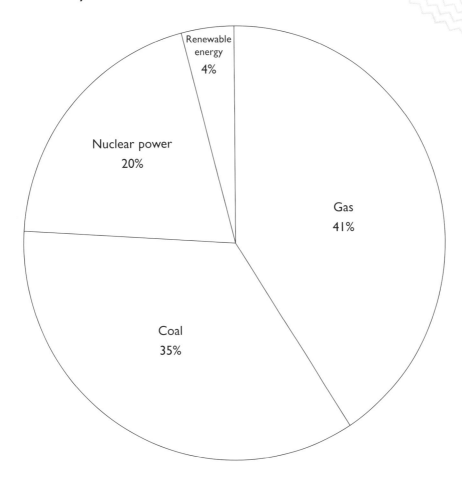

The Government is planning to reduce the amount of coal which is used to generate electricity and increase the amount of renewable energy sources. However, in the short term, gas will largely replace coal.

Your school probably uses large amounts of electricity from the national grid, but it may also use other forms of energy. Carry out research to answer the following questions:

a   How much is the annual electricity bill for your school?
b   How is the heating system of the school powered?
c   How much is the annual heating bill?
d   How many batteries does the school use?
e   Does the school have any renewable energy resources of its own, for example solar panels or a wind turbine?
f   Does the school have any energy-saving features, for example insulation, double glazing, automatic computer shut down at night?

1.4 Making Savings

a You are going to carry out research to find ways of saving energy and resources in your school. First of all, choose which area you are going to focus on. You can use an idea from the pictures below or choose one of your own.

b Before you can find ways of saving resources, you have to find out where and why they are being wasted. Make a list of:

◎ places you need to look at
◎ people you need to talk to
◎ questions you need to find answers to.

c Now carry out your research. Remember to record your findings carefully.

PLTS in PSHE: Effective Participators © Folens (copiable page)

1.5 Action Plan

Our aim _____

Action	Permission to be obtained from	Students responsible	Date to be completed			
Reduce paper sent home by using email for letters. Letter to go home to parents with reply slip for parents to choose paper or email letters. Office will need to keep list of email/paper recipients.	Head teacher and governors	Sasha and Kerry	Feb 21st			

Objectives

By the end of the lesson, students will:

◎ have identified improvements that would benefit others as well as themselves.

◎ have tried to influence others.

◎ have thought about respect and how it can improve school life.

Prior knowledge

None.

Links

Personal, Social, Health and Economic Education Programmes of Study for England: Personal wellbeing: 1.5 Diversity.

Curriculum for Excellence for Scotland: Health and wellbeing: Mental, emotional, social and physical wellbeing.

Personal and Social Education Framework for Wales: Active citizenship.

Revised Curriculum for Northern Ireland: Learning for Life and Work: Personal development.

Background

You will need copies of any documents your school has which outline expectations of students' behaviour. This might be the school's code of conduct, home school agreement or behaviour policy.

Starter activity

Read out the following definition from the Collins *Essential English Dictionary* and ask students to guess the word: 'Consideration. An attitude of deference or esteem. To pay proper attention or consideration to.' (Answer: respect).

Activity sheets

Students could work in small groups to discuss the illustrations on Activity sheet **2.1 Lack Of Respect?** and write their lists.

They will then use the lists from Activity sheet **2.1** to carry out the work on Activity sheet **2.2 More Respect**, they could do the poster activity in groups or individually.

Activity sheets **2.3 Code Of Conduct** and **2.4 Bringing It Alive** require students to look at the school's code of conduct or similar document. You could impose limits on what activities you allow. For example, you could ask that they all prepare an assembly, and then choose the best one to be presented, or ask different groups to prepare assemblies for different year groups. Wherever possible the activities should be 'real', i.e. activities which they will actually carry out within the school.

The final Activity sheet **2.5 One School's Approach** looks at wider issues, including teacher training, leadership and whole-school policies. This will give students a chance to see some of the issues from a different point of view. If issues arise from this sheet you may wish to initiate an activity where students can campaign for change. For example, they might choose to create audio files of difficult-to-pronounce names for use in staff training.

Plenary

'Respect' is a word often used in song lyrics (for example, songs by Aretha Franklin, Pink, Erasure, Pantera). How many songs can students name which are about respect? Why is it such a popular song topic?

2.1 Lack Of Respect?

a Look at the situations below. Which ones show people respecting each other and which ones show a lack of respect? How many of these happen regularly in your school?

Wednesday

Lamb Pilaff
or
Vegetable Moussaka
with
Apple Sponge &
Vanilla Sauce

b Write two lists, showing how people show respect to each other in your school and how they show a lack of respect. Keep these lists somewhere safe – you will need them later.

2.2 More Respect

Look at the lists you wrote for Activity sheet 2.1.

a   What areas to do with respect in your school do you think need improving?
It might be how people speak to each other, how they behave around school, or
how people are treated concerning their beliefs or culture. The comments below
might give you some ideas.

b   Choose one issue concerning lack of respect which you think needs to be
improved in your school and design a poster encouraging people to show
more respect over that issue.

PLTS in PSHE: Effective Participators   © Folens (copiable page)

2.3 Code Of Conduct

Your school probably has a code of conduct or a similar document which sets out expectations about student behaviour. Read a copy of this document carefully before answering the following questions.

a Have you seen this document before?

_____

b If yes, did you remember what was in it?

_____

c Has anyone ever gone through the document with you (for example, a parent, tutor or teacher)?

_____

d What kinds of behaviour would be acceptable according to this document? (Give examples)

_____

e What kinds of behaviour would be unacceptable according to this document? (Give examples)

_____

f Do you think this document makes a difference to how people behave in your school? Give reasons for your answer.

_____

2.4 Bringing It Alive

a A code of conduct, or other document about behaviour, only works if people know what's in it and try to keep to it. The students below are trying to find a way to remind people about their school's code of conduct. Look at each idea. Which ones do you think would be most effective?

b Plan and carry out a project to raise awareness of the code of conduct or behaviour policy in your school. You can use one of the ideas above or an idea of your own.

2.5 One School's Approach

When Ellen Moore took over as head teacher at her school, she was concerned about the lack of respect which people showed each other. This is how she tackled it.

When I started here, I didn't like the way people treated each other. There was a lot of shouting – teachers shouted at students and students shouted back. Students called each other names, sometimes making racist comments, and there was a lot of pushing and shoving in the corridors.

I spent the first year talking a lot about respect. In staff meetings we talked about alternatives to shouting in class and we agreed a behaviour policy with clear sanctions for those who broke it. We created a policy of walking on the left hand side and rewarded pupils who were seen acting politely in the corridors. I did assemblies about respect, put up posters and asked the PSHE department to focus on it too.

Sometimes the issues were racial. We held a multicultural week to highlight the different cultures within the school and talked about showing understanding and tolerance for other people's beliefs.

Gradually things have changed. There is now an area on the staff IT system showing teachers how to pronounce some of the more unusual student names and I expect staff to check it before they take a new class. We have included an optional headscarf as part of the uniform. There was a lot of discussion about whether or not non-Muslim girl should be allowed to wear it and whether or not crucifixes should be allowed. When I heard people expressing their opinions on these matters, and listening and considering other people's thoughts, I knew we had come a long way.

Make a list of the practical things Mrs Moore did to change the way people treated each other in the school. How do you think these things have changed the ethos of the school? Could your school learn any lessons from Mrs Moore?

Objectives

By the end of the lesson, students will:

◎ have tried to influence others, negotiating and balancing diverse views to reach workable solutions.

◎ have found out about local and national sources of support for people with concerns relating to illegal drug use.

Prior knowledge

None.

Links

Personal, Social, Health and Economic Education Programmes of Study for England: Personal wellbeing: 1.2 Healthy lifestyles.

Curriculum for Excellence for Scotland: Health and wellbeing: Substance misuse.

Personal and Social Education Framework for Wales: Health and emotional wellbeing.

Revised Curriculum for Northern Ireland: Learning for Life and Work: Personal development

Background

According to a government report 'resilience to drug use is enhanced by increasing social skills, social attachments and material resources' (*Preventative factors for illicit drug use among young people, Home Office 2005*). This means that the social skills developed through this unit, particularly through the use of role play and discussion, may be as important as the information students are learning.

Starter activity

What stories are around in the media at the moment concerning drug abuse? There may be real stories relating to celebrities or other people, or storylines in films and soaps. Do these stories act as a warning or do they glamorize drug use?

Activity sheets

Activity sheet **3.1 What Are The Dangers?** asks students to think about the variety of ways in which drugs can be responsible for deaths or injuries. Question b on this sheet gives them the opportunity to research local news stories and may need to be

done as homework. You may need to be sensitive to any recent issues concerning students at the school or their families.

Students could work in groups to discuss the comments on Activity sheet **3.2 Why Don't They Listen?** before sharing ideas as a class. Try to focus attention on the reasons why the characters' arguments are wrong. For example, the first man says that if his mental health is affected it won't affect anyone else. Clearly this is untrue; it could affect his family, friends, neighbours, work colleagues, health professionals and anyone else who comes into contact with him.

Activity sheet **3.3 A Worrying Time** will involve research. Encourage students to include a range of local and national sources of help, and formal and informal ones. For example, they might include family and friends, school counsellors, websites, charities, GPs and any specialist services in the area.

Activity sheet **3.4 Councils Get Active** introduces a role play activity. You can use Activity sheet **3.5 Drugs – Role Play Cards** to help students develop characters. Students could work in groups of about eight, or the role play could be carried out as a whole class activity where eight students take on the roles on the cards, and the others act as additional councillors, advisors and members of the public.

Plenary

Students could make copies of their leaflets from Activity sheet **3.3** and hand them out to other students. Some students could also contact their local council to find out if there are any initiatives to deal with drug abuse in the area.

3.1 What Are The Dangers?

Every year, despite plenty of warnings, people are killed or injured as a result of drug taking. Look at the stories below. How did drugs contribute to the danger in each case?

Nicola contracted the disease after sharing a needle when she was a heroin user.

Soap star found dead – drug overdose suspected

MY CHILDREN WERE TAKEN INTO CARE FOR THEIR OWN SAFETY

A 32-year-old woman, who cannot be named for legal reasons, sobbed in court today as her three children were taken into care. She admitted three counts of neglect and one of physically harming her daughter and blamed her drug addiction for her actions. 'I used to be a lovely, calm person but now I just lose my temper all the time. I know my children aren't safe with me at the moment but I will fight to get off these drugs and get them back.'

19-year-old man drowned after night out

The body of a 19-year-old man from Stockport was found in the River Goyt on Sunday morning following a police search. The man went missing after a night out with friends. Police say that low levels of alcohol were found in his blood along with a number of illegal substances.

Three injured by drug driver

Three teenagers were being treated in hospital yesterday after a car driven by a 22-year-old woman mounted the pavement and hit them. The woman has admitted to smoking marijuana before driving the car to collect her daughter from school.

In 2006 there were 2,570 deaths in England and Wales where drug use was thought to be a contributory factor. Often drug-related deaths and injuries also involve alcohol. Carry out research to find out if there have been any drug-related accidents or injuries in your area in the last year.

3.2 Why Don't They Listen?

a The people below know the dangers that drugs can pose but they still choose to take them. Look at the reasons they give. Write a reply to each one explaining why their reasons are not convincing. (Hint: think back to the stories on Activity sheet 3.1)

> It's no one else's business if I smoke pot or not. It doesn't make you harm people. I know the dangers: I know that it can make some people more likely to get mental health problems but that's my look out isn't it? It won't affect anyone else.

> I occasionally use drugs but I don't think they do you any harm as long as you don't do it too often. I don't know anyone personally who's died from drug use so it can't be that dangerous.

> I started doing drugs at school because I wanted to be different. I was fed up with being good. Now it's become a bit of a habit but I wouldn't say I was addicted. I always use the same supplier and he's never sold me any bad stuff so I know I'll be OK.

> You've got to have a bit of fun in life haven't you? Drugs are a laugh, they give you a buzz, that's why people use them. It's really no different from bungee jumping or driving racing cars and no one tries to ban that.

b Anti-drug campaigners use many different approaches to try to get people to understand the dangers of using drugs. Which of the following have you come across? Which do you think are most effective?

Giving facts   Using statistics   Personal stories   Frightening people

Shocking people   Showing the consequences   Explaining the dangers

PLTS in PSHE: Effective Participators © Folens (copiable page)

3.3 A Worrying Time

Read the comments below. Where might these people find help if they lived in your area?

My older brother uses drugs. My mum doesn't know and he says he'll kill me if I tell her.

I think my daughter is using drugs. I found a little bottle of something in her room. I don't know what it is and I don't know who to ask. I don't want the police involved.

Most of my friends use drugs. I never used to get involved but recently I lost my job. I've got nothing to do and I've been feeling really fed up. A mate gave me some speed and it felt fantastic. I've used it several times since. I know I shouldn't but what else is there in my life at the minute?

My mum and stepdad are both drug addicts. My social worker thinks they're clean at the minute but they're not. None of my friends come round anymore and I have to look after my two younger brothers so I can't go out. I don't want to say anything because we'll all get put into foster care again. Maybe they'll come off the stuff again soon.

Design a leaflet giving people advice on what to do if they have any worries about drugs. Your leaflet should include places where they can get information and help. Remember to include national and local sources of help.

Read the newspaper report below.

CRICKLESLADE

Councillor Sara Hussain has called for an extraordinary general meeting of Crickleslade Council this month after three separate incidents involving drug abuse in the area. Councillor Hussain says, 'I became alarmed when a local school had to exclude two pupils for bringing drugs into school last term. The following week I was contacted by a member of the public whose six year old daughter had found hypodermic needles underneath the swings in the park. Then just last week an ambulance attended a call on one of our housing estates where a young man had collapsed after using illegal drugs. Drug abuse is clearly a growing problem in our area and we can't ignore it any longer. I want to get the local people together so that we can talk about this problem and find a way to tackle it before something really tragic happens. I know we like to think we live in a nice area where these things don't happen but it's just not true anymore'.

A meeting will be held at 7pm on Tuesday evening at the parish hall. The meeting will be open to the public and councillors are hoping that as many people as possible from the area will attend.

Use the cards on Activity sheet 3.5 to prepare your characters, then role play the council meeting. By the end of the meeting try to have reached an agreement about at least three things that the council will do to help combat the local drug problem.

3.5 Drugs – Role Play Cards

Chairperson

You are the chairperson of the council. It is your job to make sure that everyone's opinions are heard and that the meeting reaches some sort of conclusion.

Councillor

You are an adult member of the council. You believe that a 'hard line' approach should be taken against drugs with the emphasis being on catching and punishing those people who are supplying and using drugs.

Councillor

You are an adult member of the council. You have worked with drug offenders before and you believe that many people turn to drugs as a result of other problems in their lives. You think the council should be providing support for vulnerable people.

Councillor

You are an adult member of the council. You don't believe council money should be wasted on people who have got themselves mixed up with drugs. You would rather see the money spent on local services for children and old people.

Youth Representative

You are a teenager who represents the local youth club. You know that some young people in the area are getting involved with drugs and you think the council should be doing more to help young people.

Doctor

You are the local doctor. You have noticed a sharp increase in the number of patients coming to you with drug-related problems. You would like your surgery to be involved in any anti-drug campaign that is launched.

Police Community Support Officer

You have been working in this area for two years now. You are concerned by the amount of underage drinking that goes on in the area and you believe that parents are unaware of the things their children get up to. You want the council to pay for a youth worker to work with you in the evenings and weekends, talking to youngsters and their parents.

Member of the Public

You are a member of the public. You know a number of people who use illegal drugs and none of them are under 30-years-old. You are concerned that this is being seen as a 'youth problem' when perhaps it isn't.

Teacher's Notes

Objectives

By the end of the lesson, students will:

◎ have thought about the wide variety of activities available to students, and the way in which their safety is ensured.

◎ have identified improvements that would benefit others as well as themselves.

◎ have proposed practical ways forward, breaking those down into manageable steps.

Prior knowledge

None.

Links

Personal, Social, Health and Economic Education Programmes of Study for England: Personal wellbeing: 1.5 Diversity.

Curriculum for Excellence for Scotland: Health and wellbeing: Mental, emotional, social and physical wellbeing.

Personal and Social Education Framework for Wales: Health and emotional wellbeing.

Revised Curriculum for Northern Ireland: Learning for Life and Work: Personal development.

Background

As teachers we tend to focus on lesson time at school, but for most students the time spent during break, lunch and immediately after school is equally, if not more, important. These times typically make up about 20 per cent of a student's school day. Many new students find these the most stressful times and a significant proportion of students continue to have problems coping with these less structured sessions.

Starter activity

Ask students, 'What are breaks and lunch time for?' Give students three minutes to jot down their ideas before sharing ideas as a class.

Activity sheets

In this unit students will be analysing the school and how it is used by students during breaks, lunchtime and after school. Students can work in groups of three or four, and you might want to ensure that these three different times are covered by different groups. If your school is particularly active before school you could include this time too. You might want to provide students with A3 size, black and white outline copies of a map of the school to save time. You will also need to provide details of supervision arrangements. You do not need to provide student or teacher names but students need to know the level of supervision for each area, for example how many teachers and prefects are on duty each break time, and the areas they cover.

Activity sheet **4.1 What Goes On?** asks students to think of all the activities, organised and informal, which take place out of lesson time at school. They then use this information for Activity sheet **4.2 Where Does It Happen?** to put together their 'break time map'.

Activity sheet **4.3 Who's In Charge?** looks at the level of supervision around the school and Activity sheet **4.4 Is It Enough?** evaluates whether or not provision is adequate. If the students' investigation leads to the conclusion that some changes need to be made you can then decide how to move forward from this point. Of course, you may need to remind students that their needs and wishes have to be balanced against the resources available.

Plenary

Students could use their maps as part of the induction process for new students, showing them where they can go at different times of the day. Discuss this idea with students.

a   In addition to lessons, many other things go on in your school. Use the table
    below to list all the things that students do outside lesson time. Remember to
    include organised activities such as clubs as well as things like reading, talking
    or eating lunch.

Break times	Lunchtime	After school

b   Now code each item on your list using three different colours or symbols to show
    which activities are:
    • fully supervised (e.g. a club run by a member of staff)
    • partially supervised (e.g. take place in areas of the school where members of
      staff are on duty)
    • unsupervised (e.g. take place in an area where staff rarely go).

4.2 Where Does It Happen?

You are going to produce a map of your school showing the different activities that go on during either break, lunchtime or after school. Follow the instructions below to produce your map.

1. Draw or photocopy a large map of your school. It needs to be about A3 size.

2. Decide whether you are going to focus on break time, lunchtime or after school (and note this on your map).

3. Black out any areas which are always out of bounds for students at that time.

4. If your school has certain areas for different students (e.g. a Year 7 playground or an area for prefects only) find a way of showing this on your map.

5. Look at the list of activities which you compiled for Activity sheet 4.1. You are going to show these activities on your map. Think of a sensible way to do this. You may need to use symbols or codes with a key, and you may need to group activities together under headings (e.g. eating, active games, socialising, etc).

6. Work lightly in pencil at first so you can make changes if necessary.

7. Once you have agreed a system, complete your map showing where and what students do.

8. Remember to include a key or other relevant information on your map.

4.3 Who's In Charge?

a Ask your teacher for a copy of the rota or other system used to supervise the students around the school for the time period covered by your map (see Activity sheet 4.2). This might include a staff duty rota, a prefect or monitor rota, and/or a lunchtime supervisor rota.

b Compare the rotas with your map. Which areas are heavily supervised and which areas are lightly supervised? Are there any areas in the school which are not supervised at all?

c Where would you advise the following students to go?

I like playing football with my friends but we don't really want to play with the older kids.

I've got two good friends and we like playing on computers. If we can't do that we like to stand around and talk.

I don't like a lot of noise or shoving about. I like to be somewhere quiet where a member of staff can keep an eye on me as I sometimes find it difficult to get on with other people.

4.4 Is It Enough?

a Carry out the following audit to decide whether any changes are needed in your school during the time covered by your map (break time, lunchtime or after school). You can answer the questions yourself or ask other people's opinions.

1. Are there enough organised activities for students? _____
   _____

2. Are there enough places for students to go to? _____
   _____

3. Is there enough variety of places (for example, places to be active, places to talk quietly, etc)? _____
   _____

4. Are the needs of different age groups met fairly? _____
   _____

5. Are more seating areas needed? _____
   _____

6. Are all the areas supervised adequately? _____
   _____

7. Do students feel safe everywhere? _____
   _____

8. Are there enough rubbish bins and are they in the right places? _____
   _____

b Now that you have studied what happens in your school out of lesson time, do you think any changes are needed? Write a letter to your head teacher, school council or governing body outlining your findings. If you think something needs to be added or changed, make the case for it and suggest how it could be provided.

PLTS in PSHE: Effective Participators © Folens (copiable page)

Teacher's Notes

Objectives

By the end of the lesson, students will:

◎ have identified improvements that would benefit others as well as themselves.

◎ have thought about the ways in which young people can have a positive influence in the world.

◎ have presented a persuasive case for action.

◎ have chosen actions which they can take that will be of benefit in ways that matter to them.

Prior knowledge

None.

Links

Personal, Social, Health and Economic Education Programmes of Study for England: Personal wellbeing: 1.1 Personal identities.

Curriculum for Excellence for Scotland: Social studies: People in society, economy and business.

Personal and Social Education Framework for Wales: Active citizenship.

Revised Curriculum for Northern Ireland: Learning for Life and Work: Local and global citizenship.

Background

This unit aims to show students that young people can help influence decisions and gives them some ideas of the ways in which they can influence change. Students interested in political change might like to look at the Youth Parliament website at www.ukyouthparliament.org.uk.

Starter activity

Ask students to name one thing they have done today that has made the world a better place. It might be something as small as smiling or saying thank you to the bus driver. Collect as many ideas as possible.

Activity sheets

Students could carry out the activities on Activity sheet **5.1 From Little Things** in pairs before sharing ideas as a class.

The answers for Activity sheet **5.2 Persuading Others** are not definitive, as there are different models of local government across the UK, but,

given the choices available, the answers would be 1b, 2g, 3d, 4a, 5c, 6e, 7f. You can use the exercise to highlight the issue of what different bodies control and how this affects where you go to discuss things. For example, something affecting a region as a result of a European ruling might be best dealt with by the Member for the European Parliament, although you might also involve your MP.

The final activity on this sheet might need to be done as a whole class exercise and you may need to offer prompts in the shape of scenarios. For example, who might they approach if they felt solar panels were too expensive? Answers could include the Government to ask for subsidies and the companies that produce solar panels. Other organisations to approach for a campaign might include Neighbourhood Watch schemes, local Police forces, the Advertising Standards Authority, the Commission for Racial Equality and any other groups with authority over people and regulations.

Activity sheets **5.3 Georgina's School Trip** and **5.4 Making A Difference** are designed to help students see that they really can make a difference. There could be a class discussion to share ideas about the things people could do at the end of the lesson. It will be up to students whether or not they actually do any of the things on their lists.

Activity sheet **5.5 The Pledge** can be used at the end of the unit by those students who wish to commit to it. Encourage them to be ambitious and list as many things as they want. You could collect in the pledges and give them out in a year's time to see how many of them have been fulfilled up to that point.

Plenary

Students could find out the names of their local councillor, MP and MEP.

5.1 From Little Things ...

How could putting a piece of paper on a table save someone's life? Read the following story to find out.

Cara couldn't give blood because she had an infection, but she took a leaflet about being a blood donor and left it in the staff room where she worked.

Ian saw the leaflet. He made a note of his local clinic, went along and donated blood.

Billy was born with a rare disease. He needed a blood transfusion straight away. Ian's blood saved Billy's life

Even the tiniest action can have massive effects. And if millions of people all do something tiny, the effects soon add up.

If every household in the UK replaced one standard light bulb with an energy-saving bulb, it would reduce the release of greenhouse gases by an amount equivalent to that produced in a year by 800,000 cars, according to the International Energy Agency.

If every school-aged child in the UK saved just one piece of paper each, that would be a saving of almost 38 tonnes of paper.

If every person in the UK recycled just one drinks can each, there would be approximately 22 thousand tonnes less waste to go into landfill sites.

Make a list of all the tiny things you could do which could have a massive impact for good in the world. Choose one thing which you are going to do TODAY.

PLTS in PSHE: Effective Participators

5.2 Persuading Others

a Sometimes you can simply take action yourself, but often you may need to persuade others to take action too. Look at the situations on the left below. Match them to the people or organisations you would have to persuade on the right.

1. You want to be able to cycle to school but there is no secure bike shed.	**a.** Your MP
2. You want your mum to be able to have a new cancer fighting drug which her doctor says isn't available in your area.	**b.** The school governors
3. The youth club in your village may have to close because the rent on the village hall has gone up.	**c.** The local town council
4. A family in your town are being threatened with deportation even though they have lived in the UK for 15 years and two of the children were born here.	**d.** The parish council
5. There are no facilities for recycling drinks cartons in your area.	**e.** The education department of your local authority
6. There are plans to close one of the primary schools in the area which you think should be kept open.	**f.** Your MEP
7. Your area, which relies on the fishing industry, is struggling to survive because of strict fishing quotas.	**g.** The local primary care trust

b Make a list of organisations you might approach if you were campaigning about something. Begin with the ones listed above and add any more ideas that you can think of. Think about local, national and international issues.

5.3 Georgina's School Trip

Georgina is a wheelchair user and she is also diabetic. When her school arranged a week's trip to France, Georgina was told she would not be able to go because the facilities were not suitable. Look at what happened next:

Georgina and her mum talked to the head teacher. The head teacher explained that the hotel they were staying in was not 'wheelchair friendly', and also said that she could not ask any of the teachers to be responsible for Georgina's medication. Georgina and her mum were disappointed but accepted the situation.

Georgina's friend, Becky, encouraged Georgina to take it further. Georgina phoned the hotel in France. They said that, although much of the hotel was not suitable for wheelchairs, they did have a downstairs room that Georgina could use and they would be prepared to fit a ramp to the main entrance.

Georgina spoke again to the head teacher but the head was still not happy about taking Georgina because of her diabetes. Becky contacted the governors. She also contacted the local paper.

Georgina's doctor wrote a letter to the governors explaining that Georgina was perfectly capable of monitoring her own medication and offered training to any member of staff who wanted to keep an eye on it. The governors held an emergency meeting. A member of staff volunteered to supervise Georgina.

Georgina went to France with her friends and had a wonderful time.

5.4 Making A Difference

a Read Activity sheet 5.2. What steps did Georgina and Becky take to persuade the head teacher and the governors of the school to change their minds? Was it worth the effort?

Many young people carry out effective campaigns. The following are all true stories:

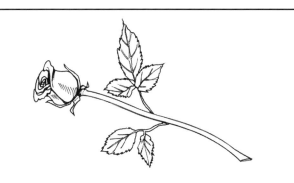

Fifteen-year-old Lizzie Mclean set up Project Rose which is an organisation run by students in schools. They sell silk roses and deliver them anonymously on Valentine's Day. The money raised goes to Breast Cancer Research. www.projectrose.co.uk

Fifteen-year-old Seb Green stole a boat and had to be rescued by helicopter off the coast at Weymouth. Seb estimated that it had cost the rescue services and hospital around £20,000 so when he was 18 he decided to pay off his debt. He spent a year walking round the coast of Britain and raised over £30,000 for the Dorset and Somerset Air Ambulance and Starlight Children's Foundation. www.sebsodyssey.org.uk/flyermk2.html

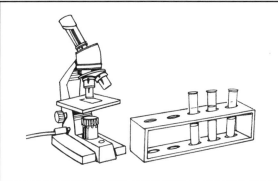

Sixteen-year-old Laurie Pycroft founded the group Pro-Test which campaigns in favour of animal testing for scientific research. Laurie became frustrated with the lack of information about the benefits of animal testing in research and wanted to provide an alternative view to the anti-testing groups. www.pro-test.org.uk/index.php

b What issues would you be prepared to make a stand for? Look at the issues in the box below. For each one, jot down three things you could do to make things better. It might be something that will help directly (such as switching off lights to save energy) or something to encourage others to make changes (such as raising money for charity).

The environment

Your local area

Animal rights

School

World poverty

c Now look at your list. Are there any things you would actually like to do? What's stopping you?

I _____

want to make this world a better place. In order to do this, I promise

that today I will _____

_____ .

Tomorrow I will _____

_____ .

I promise that in the next year I will _____

_____ .

And I promise that, over my lifetime, I will _____

_____

_____ .

I promise that I will keep this pledge to the best of my ability.

Signed _____ Date _____

Objectives

By the end of the lesson, students will:

◎ have discussed issues of concern, seeking resolutions where needed.
◎ have found out about child labour and organisations which exist to combat it.
◎ have researched ethical shopping.

Prior knowledge
None.

Links

Personal, Social, Health and Economic Education Programmes of Study for England: Economic wellbeing and financial capability: 1.4 Economic understanding.

Curriculum for Excellence for Scotland: Social Studies: People in society, economy and business.

Personal and Social Education Framework for Wales: Sustainable development and global citizenship.

Revised Curriculum for Northern Ireland: Learning for Life and Work: Local and global citizenship.

Background

Around the world approximately 246 million children are employed in child labour. This includes manufacturing goods, agricultural work, domestic work and the sex trade. For a comprehensive assessment of the problems and solutions see the UNICEF UK report *Child Labour Today* (UnicefUK 2006) which can be downloaded at www.unicef.org.uk/publications/pdf/ECECHILD2_A4.pdf

Starter activity

Take a quick straw poll to find out how many hours students in the class work each week. This can include paid work or work around the home, but not school or homework. Compare this to the 16 hour day which Sumitra in Activity sheet **6.2 Sumitra's Story** worked.

Activity sheets

The first four activity sheets in this unit focus on the work done by RugMark to reduce child labour in the rug-making industries of India, Nepal and Pakistan. Students can work through the activities on Activity sheet **6.1 What Are You Walking On?**,

referring to Activity sheets **6.2**, **6.3 About RugMark** and **6.4 Answering Back** as required. Ideally, the letter writing activity on Activity sheet **6.4** should be a real activity with students writing to local shops. They may have to carry out research to find out whether their local carpet shops already stock RugMark labelled rugs or not. Activity sheet **6.5 What Else?** broadens the issue and looks at other products which frequently use child labour.

Plenary

In the UK there are strict laws governing child labour. Consider these rules and ask students whether or not they think they are fair. You can find a summary of permitted working hours here: www.direct.gov.uk/en/YoungPeople/Workand careers/Yourrightsandresponsibilitiesatwork/DG_066 272

6.1 What Are You Walking On?

a Do you have any rugs in your home? If so, do you know where they come from? Many hand woven rugs are imported from Asia. Some are produced by reputable companies who pay their staff a decent wage, but many are made in factories where conditions are poor and wages are low. Some companies use child labour. Read Activity sheet 6.2 to find out how Sumitra was rescued from a rug factory.

b RugMark is an organisation which was set up in 1994 by a group of charities and people from the rug making industry who wanted to end child labour and improve conditions for rug workers. Read Activity sheet 6.3 to find out more about RugMark.

c Now look at the comments below. Write an answer to each one explaining why the reasons they give are not necessarily good reasons for keeping child labour.

In poor countries, children need to work to help their parents make ends meet.

It's traditional in some countries for children to work with their parents and learn a trade.

Children in poor countries need to learn a trade.

If children can't work legally, they will end up in illegal jobs, like prostitution.

d Read Activity sheet 6.4. Which of the statements given would be effective answers to the comments above?

My family lived in a tiny village in Nepal. We were very poor. When I was 7 I was sent away to work. I was sent to the city where me and three other girls lived with a man called Dharma who worked in the carpet factory. We slept on the floor in a damp room and each day we were woken at 4am to go to the rug factory to work. We worked till about nine o'clock at night, with only one meal. I never got paid. Dharma said he had given my parents money and I would have to work until I had paid off the debt. I spent all day knotting rugs with hardly any breaks. If I slowed down I got shouted at and often I got hit too.

One day a social worker from RugMark came round. Dharma tried to hide me but the social worker saw me. He asked if I would like to come with him but I said no because I didn't know who he was. Dharma told me he was a bad man, but I heard some of the other workers talking and I believed them so when the social worker came back I said I did want to go.

Now I live at the RugMark rehabilitation centre. I go to school and I am looked after and fed well. RugMark have contacted my parents and they have agreed that I can stay here until I am older. I am studying hard and I want to become a teacher. I am so happy. I didn't think I would ever be happy again.

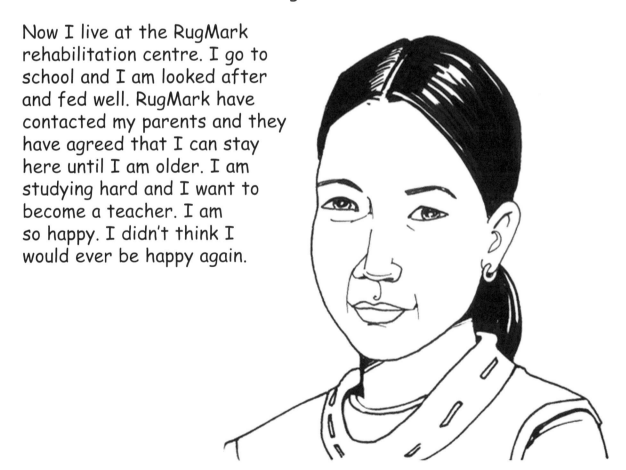

RugMark works in India, Nepal and Pakistan. Exporters pay a fee to use the RugMark label and the money is used to fund RugMark's work. Exporters can only use the label if they agree not to use illegal child labour, allow RugMark inspectors to inspect their factories and pay their workers fair wages.

Around 300,000 children work in rug factories in South Asia.

RugMark have rescued over 3,000 children. Some have been reunited with their families. Others have gone to live in RugMark rehabilitation centres where they receive food, care, education and training.

Since RugMark began in 1994 over 5.5 million rugs have been exported to North America and Europe with the RugMark label.

RUGMARK ®

CERTIFICATION NO:

053N9375   NEPAL
80*92 CM

RugMark also runs welfare projects, mobile clinics and adult education classes.

RugMark runs pre-school childcare centres so that woman can work in the rug factories without taking young children with them.

The RugMark label includes a tracking number to help guard against counterfeit labelling.

6.4 Answering Back

Sometimes people argue that child labour is inevitable in poor countries and that we will make things worse if we try to stop it. The statements below can be used to respond to the comments on Activity sheet 6.1.

Child labour keeps wages low. Adult workers are paid less in areas where children are employed because child labour drives the wages down. Adults should be paid a fair wage so that they don't have to rely on their children.

In many cultures where parents traditionally worked at home children used to help out, but as families become poorer, children can end up working longer and longer hours. They are often sent to factories without their parents where they work long hours for low wages in dangerous conditions. This is not traditional, or right.

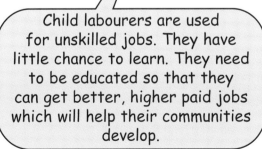

Child labourers are used for unskilled jobs. They have little chance to learn. They need to be educated so that they can get better, higher paid jobs which will help their communities develop.

It is important that, in areas where child labour is brought to an end, alternatives are provided. This means providing more free education and ensuring that parents can earn enough money to keep their children safe. People in the developed world must be prepared to pay a reasonable amount for imported goods.

Using all the information you have learnt about RugMark and the rug-making industry, write a letter to a rug retailer asking them to stock RugMark labelled rugs. Give reasons for your request.

6.5 What Else?

Estimates suggest that 246 million children around the world are engaged in child labour. Many goods are produced using child labour. Children are also used for domestic work (housework), in agriculture and in the sex trade. Carry out research to find out what products are sometimes made using child labour, and how you can ensure that the products you buy have not been made with child labour.

Some products to begin your research ...

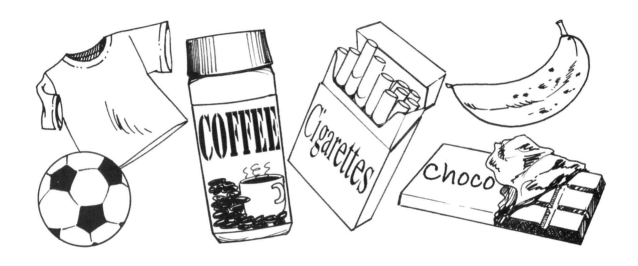

Some websites to check out ...

Traidcraft at www.traidcraftshop.co.uk

The Fairtrade Foundation at www.fairtrade.org.uk

The Clean Clothes Campaign at www.cleanclothes.org

The Ethical Consumer Magazine at www.ethicalconsumer.org

Teacher's Notes

Objectives

By the end of the lesson, students will:

◎ have acted as an advocate for views and beliefs that might be different from their own.

◎ have explored the issue of mental health and learnt to recognise warning signs when someone may need help.

◎ have found out where to go for help for mental health and emotional problems.

Prior knowledge

None.

Links

Personal, Social, Health and Economic Education Programmes of Study for England: Personal wellbeing: 1.2 Healthy lifestyles.

Curriculum for Excellence for Scotland: Health and wellbeing: Mental, emotional, social and physical wellbeing.

Personal and Social Education Framework for Wales: Health and emotional wellbeing.

Revised Curriculum for Northern Ireland: Learning for Life and Work: Personal development.

Background

Several studies suggest that as many as one in five young people suffer at some time from mental health problems. Certain groups appear to be more at risk, including looked-after children. According to the Royal College of Psychiatrists, '1 in 5 teenagers think so little of themselves that life does not seem worth living'. This unit focuses on helping students recognise the signs which might suggest that someone needs help.

Starter activity

Begin the lesson doing something completely out of character, such as standing on a chair or balancing a book on your head. Do not comment on your action. When the class laugh, or comment in any way, ask them why. Use this as an introduction to a short discussion on what we consider 'normal' behaviour and how we react when someone does something that seems 'abnormal'.

Activity sheets

Activity sheets **7.1 Is It An Eating Disorder?** and **7.2 Is It A Drink Problem?** both look at what is 'harmless' behaviour and what may be a cause for concern. You could choose the topic which you think is most relevant to your class, or you could divide the class in two and cover both topics, allowing time at the end for the two groups to show their work to each other. There is no definitive order for the statements and they are designed to provoke discussion. Students could work in pairs or groups before sharing their ideas.

Students could discuss the cases on Activity sheet **7.3 Phobia Or Foible?** in groups before sharing ideas as a class. You might want to get some of the students to look up the definitions of 'foible' and 'phobia' as well.

Activity sheet **7.4 Carrie's New Friends** should provoke a detailed discussion. Some aspects of Carrie's behaviour may be typical of many teenagers, but other aspects are clearly causes for concern, although this behaviour may be something she will simply grow out of. Encourage students to see both Carrie's and her dad's point of view, and focus on the warning signs that might suggest an ordinary interest is becoming a problem.

Activity sheet **7.5 You Don't Have To Decide** is a practical activity which students can do for homework, although the final questions should be discussed in class. Both scenarios could possibly end in disaster; it might be argued that talking to the counsellor might tip Jason's friend 'over the edge'. Students will have to weigh up the risk of doing something against that of doing nothing.

Plenary

Sometimes a mental health problem warrants a 999 call. You should call 999 only in an emergency. An emergency is defined nationally where there is:

• A danger to life
• Use of, or immediate threat of, violence
• Serious injury to a person and/or
• Serious damage to property.

7.1 Is It An Eating Disorder?

The statements below all cover eating habits. Some are more harmful than others. Arrange them in order, beginning with the least harmful and ending with the most harmful.

Eating when you're not hungry.	Eating until you feel sick.
Skipping a meal to try to lose weight.	Counting calories and keeping to a daily limit.
Making yourself sick to try to lose weight.	Refusing to eat anything containing sugar.
Drinking water before a meal so that you don't eat too much.	Going all day without eating, several times a week.
Fasting for one day.	Wanting to lose weight even though your weight is average for your height.

Keep your statements in order and answer the following questions:

a   At what point would you begin to worry about the person concerned?

b   When might you talk to them about it?

c   What other warning signs might you look for?

d   When might you seek outside help?

e   Who would you speak to?

7.2 Is It A Drink Problem?

The statements below all cover drinking habits in adults. Some are more harmful than others. Arrange them in order, beginning with the least harmful and ending with the most harmful.

Lying about how much you drink.	Drinking one or two drinks, every day of the week.
Binge drinking until you are sick on one occasion.	Regularly binge drinking until you are sick or feel very drunk.
Drinking on your own.	Drinking because it makes you feel better.
Drinking one or two drinks, once or twice a week.	Drinking in secret.
Spending money that you should be using for other things on drink.	Losing your temper when you drink.

Keep your statements in order and answer the following questions:

a At what point would you begin to worry about the person concerned?

b When might you talk to them about it?

c What other warning signs might you look for?

d When might you seek outside help?

e Who would you speak to?

7.3 Phobia Or Foible?

All of these people behave in what might be seen as an 'odd' way. Which of them, if any, have a problem?

I like my bedroom to be very tidy. My CDs are in alphabetical order and all my drawers are labelled because everything I own belongs in a specific place. I vacuum every day and dust once a week. My mum laughs at me and says she wishes my brothers were the same. I don't mind about the rest of the house, but I can't sleep unless my room is immaculate.

I like school, I have lots of friends and I'm generally pretty happy, but I do have a thing about clean hands. I wash them about twenty times a day, especially if I've been somewhere with lots of people. At school I try not to touch the desks and door handles and if someone borrows a pen I can't use it again until I've washed it. I don't mind getting muddy in football but I wash my hands straight afterwards. I hate doing things like javelin, where you have to touch things other people have touched. My teacher lets me take wet wipes out with me and I wear gloves if I'm in the relay team.

I like routines and I get anxious if they are disrupted. Once the train I usually catch was replaced by a bus and I had to go home because I couldn't manage that. I shop at the same place at the same time every week and mostly buy the same things. At home my routine is fixed but I live on my own so it's not a problem. Every week I try to do one thing I haven't done before, like walk home a different way or buy a different paper. I don't always manage it but I always try because I don't want to get to the point where I can't cope with anything new.

I used to like living here but lately the neighbours have started giving me funny looks. I know they talk about me behind my back even though they are friendly to my face. I think the lady next door is stealing my post. This is making me really miserable because it happened where I lived before and I had to move. I thought things would be OK here.

As a general rule, strange habits become a problem if they are worrying you, causing you harm or if they begin to interfere with the rest of your life. Design a poster giving people advice on what to do if they are worried about their own, or a friend's, behaviour.

7.4 Carrie's New Friends

Carrie's dad is worried about her. Read the comments below.

Carrie used to be bright and cheerful, with lots of friends. She was always on the phone or going out. In the last year she has changed. She hardly ever goes out, and spends all her time on the computer. She says her old friends bore her and she'd rather spend time online with people she's met on the Internet. She has promised me she won't arrange to meet them without telling me, but she closes down the page whenever I walk in and won't talk to me about any of them. She dresses differently now too; tatty black clothes and loads of make up. When she's not on the computer she is miserable and quiet, but when she is on it I often hear her laughing hysterically or singing loudly. It's like her personality has changed completely. I try not to pry but I did check her computer once when she was out. She'd cleared the history though, so I didn't find anything out.

I can't stand my old friends any more; they just seem so childish. In fact, I can't remember the last time I enjoyed being with anyone at school. I talk to a whole group of people over the Internet now, who I have much more in common with. I'm not stupid, I know you get some nutters on the Internet, but you can usually spot them a mile off. It's not like I'm up to anything illegal, we just talk about life and death and things that really matter, instead of clothes and dumb celebrities. My friends on the Internet really understand me. I can tell them anything. If I do decide to meet any of them I will be sensible. I'll tell dad and meet them in a public place. I don't think I will meet them though. I think it would spoil things.

Make a list of the things that are worrying Carrie's dad. Now write down the things that Carrie has said which might be a cause for concern. In pairs, role play a conversation between Carrie and her dad where they explore whether or not Carrie has a problem.

7.5 You Don't Have To Decide

Fortunately, if you are worried about someone's emotional state or mental health, you don't have to make a decision about whether they need help or not. If you are at all concerned, you can refer the matter to someone who may be in a better position to assess the situation.

a Complete the chart below with the names and contact details of at least three people or organisations in each column that you could go to for help if you were worried about a friend or member of your family.

People you could speak to at home or school	Local organisations or services	National organisations or services

b Read Jason's comment below:

◎ What's the worst that could happen if Jason talks to the school counsellor about his friend?

◎ What's the worst that could happen if Jason doesn't talk to the school counsellor about his friend?

My mate seems really miserable and he keeps doing dangerous stuff but I know he'll hate me if I tell anyone. I don't know what to do.

PLTS in PSHE: Effective Participators   © Folens (copiable page)

Objectives

By the end of the lesson, students will:

◎   have identified improvements that would benefit others as well as themselves.

◎   have proposed practical ways forward, breaking these down into manageable steps.

◎   have presented a persuasive case for action.

◎   have gained an understanding of some of the health and safety issues within the school.

Prior knowledge

None.

Links

Personal, Social, Health and Economic Education Programmes of Study for England: Personal wellbeing: 1.3 Risk.

Curriculum for Excellence for Scotland: Health and wellbeing: Mental, emotional, social and physical wellbeing.

Personal and Social Education Framework for Wales: Health and emotional wellbeing.

Revised Curriculum for Northern Ireland: Learning for Life and Work: Local and global citizenship.

Background

You will need copies of any school health and safety policies for this unit. The main body regulating health and safety is the Health and Safety Executive whose web address is www.hse.gov.uk.

Starter activity

Write the title 'School science experiments' on the board and draw two columns. In one column list the advantages of practical experiments, in the other list the possible risks. Look at the risks and talk about the equipment and procedures that are in place to minimise the risks. Introduce the idea that risks are inevitable in all walks of life, and that health and safety is not about eradicating risk, but about reducing it to reasonable levels.

Activity sheets

All of the cartoons on Activity sheet **8.1 Myths And Reality** are myths. The first three are not rulings made by the Health and Safety Executive, and any schools which do follow these rules have

made the decision themselves. In the case of the fourth cartoon, according to the Health and Safety Executive no teachers have been personally sued for compensation in at least the last five years (although a handful have been prosecuted for very serious incidents).

Activity sheet **8.2 The Real Issues** prepares students for the audit which they will carry out using Activity sheet **8.3 The Audit**. You might want to divide the class up to cover different areas and aspects of the school, and you will need to think about when it would be convenient for students to visit those places.

Activity sheet **8.4 Dealing With The Issues** leads students through the process of resolving the issues step by step.

The final Activity sheet **8.5 Sitting Pretty** has been included as a resource to use with students who use computers for long periods. It is probable that the computers used by students at school are not set up to these specifications, but as students probably only use them for short periods at school this is not a problem. Students may, however, wish to take the information home and apply it to their work spaces there.

Plenary

Despite popular belief, the Health and Safety Executive rarely bans any activities. Are there any activities which students think should be banned in schools, or on school trips, on safety grounds?

8.1 Myths And Reality

Many people feel that concerns about health and safety have taken over the world and we are no longer allowed to do anything remotely dangerous. Which of the following are true and which are myths?

Schools are no longer allowed to use toilet roll tubes for model making because of the risk of infection.

School staff are not allowed to put plasters on students unless they are medically trained and have written permission from parents.

Children must not play conkers on school grounds unless they are wearing safety goggles.

When a child has an accident in school, however small, the teacher in charge is often sued.

Your school probably has a statement about health and safety. Find out who is responsible for health and safety in your school and ask them for a copy of the policy.

     PLTS in PSHE: Effective Participators   © Folens (copiable page)

8.2 The Real Issues

Use the chart below to record some of the things which need to be done to ensure health and safety in your school. Some ideas have been included to get you started. You can use the spaces at the bottom of the chart to include ideas which don't fit elsewhere.

Floors	**Furniture**
Computers	**Lighting**
Electrical equipment Needs testing regularly to check if safe.	**Food**
Vehicles	**Emergency equipment** Fire notices should be clearly displayed.

8.3 The Audit

You are going to carry out a health and safety audit of your school. First, decide which area you are going to focus on. This may be a physical space (e.g. the playground) or a particular issue (e.g. how computers are used). You can use any of the ideas already noted on Activity sheet 8.2 or use an idea of your own.

a   In the box below, write down the focus of your audit:

b   Think about the things you need to look out for during your audit and remember to consider different conditions. For example, do different issues arise if it is raining or dark; or at break time or during lessons? Does it depend on who is using the area?

c   Now carry out your audit by going to the places you are focusing on. Use the space below to write down any concerns you have about health and safety in that area.

Your health and safety audit may have raised a number of issues. Use the chart below to help you decide what you need to do about those issues. Once you have decided on your course of action – do it.

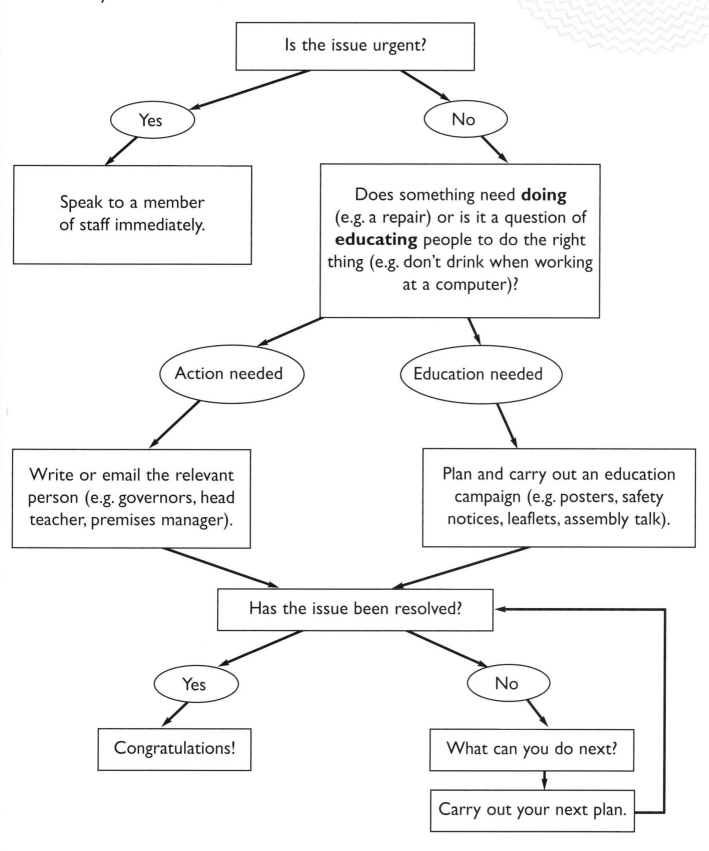

Is the issue urgent?

Yes → Speak to a member of staff immediately.

No → **Does something need doing** (e.g. a repair) or is it a question of **educating** people to do the right thing (e.g. don't drink when working at a computer)?

Action needed → Write or email the relevant person (e.g. governors, head teacher, premises manager).

Education needed → Plan and carry out an education campaign (e.g. posters, safety notices, leaflets, assembly talk).

Has the issue been resolved?

Yes → Congratulations!

No → What can you do next? → Carry out your next plan.

Look at the diagram below to see how a computer workstation should ideally be set up.

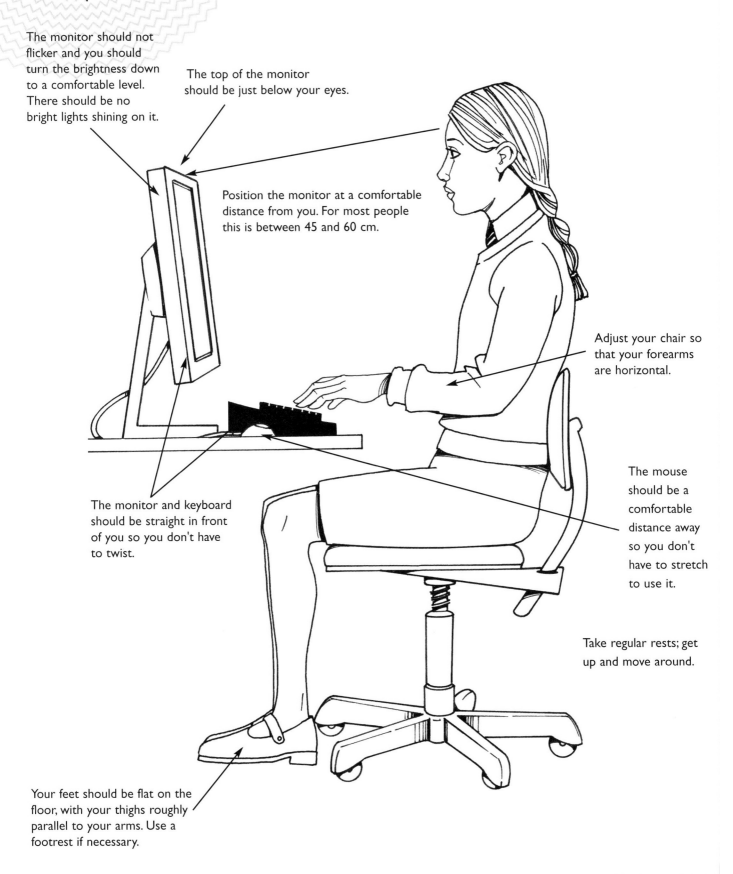

The monitor should not flicker and you should turn the brightness down to a comfortable level. There should be no bright lights shining on it.

The top of the monitor should be just below your eyes.

Position the monitor at a comfortable distance from you. For most people this is between 45 and 60 cm.

Adjust your chair so that your forearms are horizontal.

The monitor and keyboard should be straight in front of you so you don't have to twist.

The mouse should be a comfortable distance away so you don't have to stretch to use it.

Take regular rests; get up and move around.

Your feet should be flat on the floor, with your thighs roughly parallel to your arms. Use a footrest if necessary.

Objectives

By the end of the lesson, students will:

◎ have acted as an advocate for views and beliefs that may differ from their own.

◎ have learnt about the role of an advocate and how to go about finding one.

Prior knowledge
None.

Links

Personal, Social, Health and Economic Education Programmes of Study for England: Personal wellbeing: 1.4 Relationships.

Curriculum for Excellence for Scotland: Health and wellbeing: Planning for choices and changes.

Personal and Social Education Framework for Wales: Health and emotional wellbeing.

Revised Curriculum for Northern Ireland: Learning for Life and Work: Personal development.

Background

The term 'advocate' in this unit refers to a person who supports another person or group of people to try to ensure that their opinions and wishes are heard. In Scotland an advocate is a type of lawyer similar to an English barrister. This is not the type of advocate we are referring to. For more information on advocacy in the UK see the UK Advocacy Network (UKAN) website at www.u-kan.co.uk. Barnardo's run a number of projects offering advocacy for children and young people (see www.barnardos.org.uk).

Starter activity

Ask students if they have ever been in a situation where they were too frightened or nervous to speak up for themselves. What would have helped?

Activity sheets

Activity sheet **9.1 What Is Advocacy?** introduces the idea that an advocate is someone who helps another person to get their point of view heard. Students could work in pairs or small groups here.

For the role play exercise on Activity sheet **9.2 An Advocate In Action** you will also need Activity sheet **9.3 Advocacy Role Play Cards**. The simplest way to organise this activity would be to choose three students who you feel would play the roles well. Allow all the class to read the background information, then give the three students the role play cards to prepare their parts. The student playing the tutor should not see either of the other cards, but the advocate needs to read the student's card. Carry out the first role play between the student and the tutor in front of the class. Then, after sending the tutor away, carry out the role play between the student and the advocate where they decide what they are going to say. The tutor can then come back in for the final role play. The rest of the class should observe the role plays and make notes. They could also make suggestions before the final interview about how the advocate might act.

Activity sheet **9.4 What Do Advocates Do?** could be used either before or after the role play exercise to reinforce the role of an advocate.

Activity sheet **9.5 Finding An Advocate** will require research and could be set as a homework activity.

Plenary

Ask students to list the qualities needed to be a good advocate.

a Look at the situations below. What do they have in common?

Sam broke a vase and his mum got cross. As a punishment she said that he couldn't go to the rugby match the next day. She wouldn't listen to Sam. Later, Sam's older brother, Kyle, talked to their mum. He explained that the vase was broken by accident. Sam's mum agreed to listen to Sam who offered to pay for the vase. His mum let him go to the match after all.

Gordon was about to be evicted from his flat. He was behind with the rent and had upset the neighbours with his loud music. Gordon finds it difficult to talk to people and gets frustrated because he can't explain what he means when he is anxious. Ben, a support worker from MIND, went to the meeting with him. He helped Gordon explain that he was being treated for depression and that he had had problems claiming his benefits which were now sorted. Gordon listened to the housing officer and agreed to turn his music down and keep the flat tidy. Having Ben there helped Gordon to stay calm and say what he wanted. The housing officer agreed to give Gordon a month's trial.

An advocate is a person who supports someone and helps them express what they want to say. Sometimes an advocate will speak on their behalf, but mostly they are there to make sure the person can speak for themselves.

b List all the reasons why someone might find it difficult to say what they want to say.

c Consider each of the groups below and explain why they might find it particularly difficult to get their point of view across.

Young people

Carers

People with English as a second language

Elderly people

People with learning difficulties

PLTS in PSHE: Effective Participators © Folens (copiable page)

You are going to carry out a role play exercise in three parts using the cards from Activity sheet 9.3. Follow the instructions below.

Background – all participants should read this section

One of the students in the second term of the animal care course at college is causing concern. The student's attendance was quite poor in the first half of the term and the student was warned that this was unacceptable. Attendance improved for a while but seems to have declined again; the student has been absent for three days in the last month. The student is behind with two assignments. The other assignments have been completed to a good standard, but teachers report that the student sometimes seems to lack concentration in class and never joins in discussions.

Part One

Role play the interview between the student and the personal tutor, without the advocate present. Try to make the situation as realistic as possible.

Part Two

Imagine that the student has not yet been interviewed by the personal tutor. The student has been offered the services of an advocate. Role play a meeting between the student and the advocate where they decide on the main things they want to get across in the forthcoming interview. Make sure the tutor does not hear this discussion.

Part Three

Replay the interview between the student and the personal tutor, with the advocate present to support the student. Remember, the advocate is there to help the student get across the points they have agreed need to be made.

Now make notes on the following:
◎ What difference did the advocate make to the outcome?
◎ What did the advocate do that helped?
◎ Did the advocate do anything that didn't help?

The personal tutor

You are a personal tutor at a college. Having spoken to the other teachers, you have decided that this student is not committed to the course and you are going to ask the student to leave. You are a reasonable person but you don't like wasting time and you are not interested in excuses. You have a busy day and want to get this over with as quickly as possible. As far as you are concerned, this student has had their chance and you can't see any reason why they should be given another one.

The student

You are 17 years old. Until last year you were living with foster carers but two weeks into the course you were moved into a flat. At first you found it very difficult to budget, cook and organise your life but you feel you are getting better at it. Recently, however, someone moved in to the flat next to yours. Your neighbour is very noisy and last month you got practically no sleep. You are very shy and find it incredibly difficult to talk to people. You are also quite proud and you do not like talking about your personal circumstances. Your dream is to work with animals and you have found the course fascinating so far. You are really looking forward to doing the work experience next month. You are dreading seeing your tutor because you know you are behind with your work and have missed some lectures. You think you may be asked to leave and you know that you will probably clam up and say very little.

The advocate

You are an advocate who has been asked to support a student who is causing concern. Read the student's role play card. Your job is to help the student explain the situation to the tutor. You need to be firm, but polite. You can interrupt the tutor if you feel you need to, and prompt the student. For example, you could say 'We don't want to make excuses but we think it would help if you knew a little bit about (name of student)'s personal circumstances.' Then turn to the student and let them explain. Be encouraging and start them off or add things if you need to, but try to let the student do most of the talking. At the end you should ask the student 'Is there anything else you want to say?'

Fill in the gaps using the word bank below.

An advocate supports someone, or a group of people, to make sure that their _____ are heard. They do _____ give advice. They may give information but they do not tell the person they are supporting what to do. Advocates do not give their own opinions, make _____ or agree things with other people. Advocates can be _____. For example, they may be bilingual or know sign language, or they may have specialist legal _____. An advocate does not have to be a professional; they might be a _____ or simply a friend that you want to take along with you because you know they will _____ you. An advocate should always be _____. For example, if you are making a complaint against a hospital, you would not use an _____ of the hospital as your advocate. A peer advocate is someone who has something in common with the person they are supporting. For example, a person who _____ to the UK several years ago and has settled here might act as an advocate for people who have just arrived.

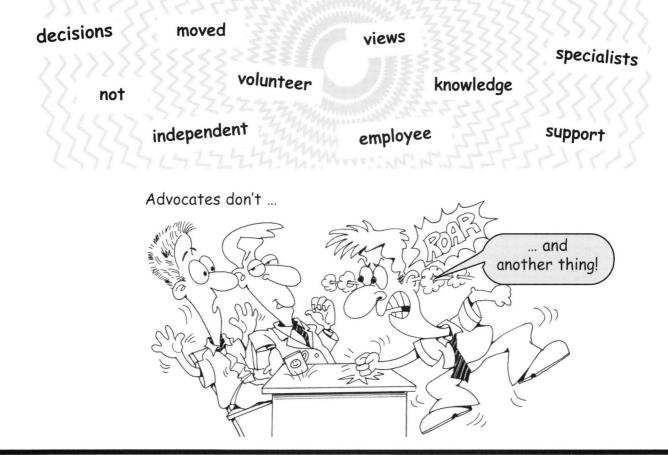

decisions   moved   views

                                          specialists

          volunteer   knowledge
  not

    independent   employee   support

Advocates don't …

ROAR

… and another thing!

a Read the scenarios below. For each one, suggest where the person might go to find an advocate. You may need to carry out research and a good place to start is the UK Advocacy Network's website at www.u-kan.co.uk. Remember there are many local and national groups offering advocacy services, and in some situations friends, volunteers or neighbours may be the best answer.

Adam is 19 and works for a garden centre. He made a complaint because he felt one of his bosses was bullying him. He has since been sacked. Adam is looking for someone to support him in his case for unfair dismissal.

Gerry's daughter has special needs. He wants her to go to a private special school which he believes has the facilities to help her learn. His local authority won't fund it, but he doesn't feel the school they want to send her to is right for her. Gerry is finding the whole appeals system confusing and wants someone to help guide him through the process.

Angela lives 400 miles away from her parents. Her mother has Alzheimer's disease and her father is partially deaf. Her parents aren't being given the help they need, although Angela suspects that the NHS and social services have offered the support and her parents are just not replying to letters and phone calls. Angela wants to find an advocate who will help sort things out.

Wicksted Comprehensive used to be a boys school but they now take girls too. At the moment only Year 7 has female students. The head teacher is concerned that the girls are not being treated equally. For example there are only two girls on the school council, and the books in the library reflect boys' tastes, as do the clubs and activities on offer. The head wants to find an advocate to encourage the girls to have a greater say in what goes on.

b If you needed support in sorting out a situation, where could you find an advocate locally? Write down three sources of help, including at least one organisation in your local area.

PLTS in PSHE: Effective Participators © Folens (copiable page)

Teacher's Notes

Objectives

By the end of the lesson, students will:

◎ have identified skills used by effective participators in other areas, including in and beyond school.

◎ have reflected on the need for effective participation as adults within the workplace and the wider community.

Prior knowledge

Awareness of skills used by effective participators as developed through previous units.

Links

Personal, Social, Health and Economic Education Programmes of Study for England: Personal wellbeing: 1.1 Personal identities.

Curriculum for Excellence for Scotland: Health and wellbeing: Planning for choices and changes.

Personal and Social Education Framework for Wales: Health and emotional wellbeing.

Revised Curriculum for Northern Ireland: Learning for Life and Work: Personal development.

Background

This unit could be used after several of the previous units have been covered, as a way of making links between PSHE lessons, other areas within the school and the wider community. You could ask other teachers to highlight effective participation within their own subjects.

Starter activity

Ask students to think of ways that they might 'leave the world a better place than they found it'.

Activity sheets

Discuss Activity sheet **10.1 In School** to help students begin to identify examples of effective participation. Ask them to match each picture with one or more of the skills listed, then suggest other examples.

They can then take Activity sheet **10.2 Evidence** away with them and fill it in over a period of about a week to gather real life examples of when they are required to be effective participators at school. The evidence collected could be used to make a display for an open evening.

Activity sheet **10.3 Beyond School** focuses on situations where people in the wider community seek to bring about change through effective participation.

Plenary

Ask the students to imagine they have to give an award to someone who they consider to be an effective participator. It can be someone students know or a famous person. Discuss nominations for the award and vote for a winner.

Identify which skills each of the effective participators below display.

I don't agree with this proposal but the class voted for it so I'll put forward their views.

Look. We'll sit down after the game and talk about the problem, but right now you two have to work together. We've got a match to win.

Skills for effective participators

◎ Discussing issues of concern, seeking resolutions where needed.

◎ Presenting a persuasive case for action.

◎ Proposing practical ways forward, breaking these down into manageable steps.

◎ Identifying improvements that would benefit others as well as themselves.

◎ Trying to influence others, negotiating and balancing diverse views to reach workable solutions.

◎ Acting as an advocate for views and beliefs that may differ from their own.

© Qualifications and Curriculum Authority

Would you like me to come and talk to your tutor with you?

Sir, we could have a rota for litter picking.

PLTS in PSHE: Effective Participators   © Folens (copiable page)

Use this sheet to record examples of when you use effective participation skills in school.

Effective participation skills	Lesson	
Discuss issues of concern, seeking resolutions where needed		
Present a persuasive case for action		
	Science	

Read the following newspaper article:

Mrs Peng knew no one when she moved onto Magden Estate

Being lonely is a feeling Jinan Peng knows only too well, and she is determined that no one in her local area will have to suffer like she did five years ago. Jinan moved to the area with her husband when he started a new job. She spent many hours alone in her flat or walking around the estate. She says, 'People were friendly and they smiled, but my English wasn't very good and I was shy.'

It was only when she met another newcomer, Alison Carls, that she decided to do something about it. 'Alison and I got talking at the shops and we realised there must be lots of lonely people about. We started by putting leaflets through doors inviting people to a coffee morning. On the first day, fourteen people turned up at my flat.'

Since then the project has grown and now the group, New Faces, meets once a fortnight in the community centre. 'I persuade people to donate things and we hold sales to cover the cost of coffee and biscuits. We keep an eye out for houses which have been sold or newly rented and someone pops round with a leaflet inviting them to the next coffee morning. I've made lots of friends through New Faces and so have other people. Sometimes people come along who've lived here for years but feel they don't know anyone. Everyone's welcome.'

a Look at the skills needed for effective participation on Activity sheet 10.1. How has Jinan Peng used each one?

b Create a display of stories from local and national newspapers showing examples of people being effective participators. You could colour code the six skills and annotate the stories accordingly.

PLTS in PSHE: Effective Participators